The Seed
in
My Nutshell

Jeanette Humphrey

ISBN 979-8-89130-490-1 (paperback)
ISBN 979-8-89130-491-8 (digital)

Christian Faith Publishing
832 Park Avenue
Meadville, PA 16335
www.christianfaithpublishing.com

Printed in the United States of America

I know a seed is tiny in comparison to a nutshell of any kind. But we are tiny when we come into this world in comparison to our full adult size. Now as I reflect on all those times in between—wow, the ups and downs, the happy and sad, the sick and well, the single and married, the working and unemployed, the family planning and having a baby or being pregnant and miscarriage—it is all such a journey with a lot of crooks and turns that can change even the best planned out dreams.

Growing up in the '50s and '60s was such an innocent time. I was one of three children, with my two older brothers being four and five years older. Even though they were close in age, they were very different in personality. Doyle, the oldest, was an entrepreneurial type with a hard work ethic. As a kid, he was always mowing yards and running a paper route, or pulling something home, he would find in-yard trash around the neighborhood and would make something new out of it. Royal, on the other hand, being seventeen months younger, was a very social spirit, always a fan of the girls, with a charming, fun, and giving personality and the good looks to go along with it. So he decided to quit high school, and with his two best buddies, he joined the Navy to serve our country and see the world. I, on the other hand, being the only girl in the family and also on my father's side of all boys, was the first granddaughter and a bit of a tomboy. So it was outdoors with Hula-Hoops, key skates, stilts, and bikes with a lot of the neighborhood kids, to mention a few.

Mom was home, and Dad worked. So we lived a very modest lifestyle. I had more home-sewn dresses than store-bought and a pair of school shoes and Sunday shoes, and then it was barefooted or flip-flops. Mom was a great home cook, making everything from scratch. So that kept our grocery bills down. I went to the Laundromat with my parents for a long time until we finally got a washing machine, and Mom would hang the clothes out to dry. She always gave special treatment to some dress shirts with starch and a lot of ironing in those days to make sure we all looked wrinkle-free and nice. We had an exhaust fan that pulled all the hot air out of the house. I honestly do not ever remember being hot without air-conditioning in those days, and that is in Florida. It was homework, piano lessons, and limited television with only a few channels. But I had my *Howdy Doody* magic screen and my record player, which I loved, especially Jerry Lee Lewis's song "Great Balls of Fire" from 1957, which was only the beginning of my love for rock and roll. Well, I have to say it ran a close race with my love for chocolate malt balls and my grandmother's six-layer chocolate cake.

We took a lot for granted in those days, with Mom running our home like a well-oiled machine and Dad's hard work ethic as a loyal employee for Standard Oil Company for over thirty-five years. It was a tradition in our family to sit down every evening together after all our long days and eat a wonderful home-cooked meal with Dad blessing the food we were about to eat. Eating out in those days was a real rarity. I would ride my bike to Dairy Queen on occasion or the local drug store soda fountain for Cherry Coke, which was so good. Of course, There was also an A&W frosted mug that was really a special treat on a hot summer day.

My parents were not only hardworking and loyal people; they were also loyal to the community church. We were always taken to Sunday school and church while growing up. And that is where I first heard the phrase "faith of a mustard seed." In those days, young girls wore charm bracelets. I had one with a lot of cute charms on it, like bowling pins, records, and typewriters, to name a few. As time went on, I added several more that would represent a special time in my life growing up. One of them was a little glass ball that had a mustard seed in it, which represented the biblical saying, "Faith of a mustard seed."

One night, at age sixteen, while washing the dishes with curlers in my hair, I got a phone call from a friend of mine wanting me to ride with her and her cousin Ted to a popular store called Rosenblum's. In those days, it was a fad to wear madras clothing, and that was the store that carried the best selections. Since my hair was still wet, I told her I would ride with her but would wait in the car for her. Well, little did I know that her cousin would decide to wait with me. That was the beginning of our getting to know each other, curlers and all. After that, we started dating. He was two years older than me and hardworking, well-dressed, with a great personality, and very kind. He was the oldest of eight children. Ted's father was disabled, and the family's income was very low. They had a large garden, fished in a local pond for fresh fish, and got government commodities, but still, ten people living in one house on very little was a challenge. This was an unhappy and frustrating conversation for him, as he was the oldest child, so he felt obligated to quit school and move in with some relatives to get a decent-paying job to help his siblings stay in school. I felt the determination and drive he had to help his family to lighten their load.

Well, as time went on, and even though I had dated others because I was still in high school, we ended up in a steady relationship. I graduated high school, and with no college plans, I started working at the Federal Reserve Bank in downtown Jacksonville. I loved this job. It was my first job out of high school, and so many other graduates from other schools also worked there. So it was great to meet and make new friends. Downtown was bustling then with so many great shops, especially shoes and dress shops, that I loved. Of course, there were parties every weekend with all the new friends. Those were the fun times. No drunken parties, and guys were, for the most part, very respectful, and the music was great. Ted was busy working in the construction trade, mostly tile installation. So he had a nice dark Florida tan to go along with his blond hair. The girls always teased me about having another date with Troy Donahue, a well-known actor back in those days who was also blond, tall, and handsome, and all the girls just loved him, and Ted resembled him a lot. Tall, dark, tanned, polite, hardworking—yeah, he was definitely getting more of my attention. We started going to church together, and Ted joined the church and was baptized. One day, while sitting in his old 58 Chevy, we began to talk more about our futures, and we came up with a young couple's dream of a brick home in the country, two children, hopefully, a boy and a girl. Of course, the boy's name would have to be Troy we laughed. I mean, what else could it be, right!

Well, it wasn't much longer until we knew this was going to be our future together, and so Ted wanted to talk to my father. You see, in those days, it was tradition and the respectful thing to do for the young man to ask the father of the girl he wanted to marry for her hand in marriage. So I told Dad that Ted wanted to talk to him. He responded with, "Do you know why?" I just shrugged my shoulders and smiled. So Dad, being the fun-loving person he was, set up a time and got the highest-watt light bulb he could find and his shotgun to clean and positioned their little talk just perfectly. He wanted Ted to sweat under that light bulb and be threatened by him cleaning his shotgun. He was the oldest brother out of six, and they were always planning out a funny story to tell each other, ha! Another good attribute of Ted's, thankfully, is that he had a good sense of humor!

So needless to say, the wedding plans did move forward. Oh, I have to say, on those wonderful downtown shopping days, I found and bought the perfect wedding dress. We were married in our church with lots of friends and family in attendance on August 11, 1967. I was only eighteen years old, and Ted was twenty. Just two young people in love with a dream and the faith of a mustard seed as they started their journey together as husband and wife.

After a honeymoon in Gatlinburg, Tennessee, we moved into an apartment. I still worked at my same job, but Ted changed to another job working for a well-known advertising company with a little more stability in pay. Although we really liked our apartment, Ted's friend, a past employer in the tile trade, offered us the little house that he and his wife were selling, and as a wedding gift, he would put a down payment on it for us. So we moved into this very small two bedroom, with an eat-in kitchen, house that was badly in need of fixing up. What fun we had with my dad painting, my brother installed new flooring, and I wallpapered and hung adorable curtains. Soon, it looked like a charming little beginner house. In a few months, Ted was advanced to supervisor with a very good increase in salary, but he missed the tile installation business. He decided he wanted to start his own company. So he opened Humphrey Tile Company and employed several of his brothers. As brothers go, that was a challenge in itself all the way around. Ted was bossy, and since he was the oldest, he felt that he could and should be in control. Well, even though that was a rough road for them all, they stuck it out and learned that they could work together even though they fought a lot. His brothers were all smart and very good at everything they did. So it wasn't long before they could venture out into their own moneymaking ventures.

With our first home finished and furnished and both of us working in great jobs, guess you can imagine the next great thing to happen. Yes, I was pregnant. Ted was doing commercial jobs out of town a lot, so toward the end of my pregnancy, I would go stay with my parents. Well, that turned out to be a good thing because our little baby boy Troy decided to enter this world three weeks early. Ted rushed home from Tallahassee, where he had a crew working on a McDonald's job. We were both amazingly happy and felt so blessed that our little baby boy Troy, who was part of our dream, had arrived.

Well, just when I thought life was perfect, we were faced with the beginning of seeing another side of life. The one that comes anytime, especially when we least expect it. You see, Ted came in from work one day and seemed puzzled as to why his right hand was not working very well. It was very slow to open and close, especially when he got really overheated or tired at work, which was a lot. So we made an appointment with his doctor, who immediately sent him to a neurologist specialist. After a number of tests, it was determined that Ted had an arterial venous malformation of the brain. That is a congenital defect that is a mass of arteries and veins that are malformed and can cause constricted blood flow to certain areas of the brain. It was located next to the main brain stem, which made it a risky surgery at that time. We were both very distraught but glad to know what it was. His doctor recommended that he not lift anything that weighed over forty pounds and not do a lot of strenuous jobs. Of course, my emotions were sad, afraid, and at an emotional standstill. Ted's mindset was scared, depressed, and what do I do now? He was a smoker and began to smoke more from the anxiety he was feeling, which was not good for him but a crutch that so many of us go to in anxious times. Some people go to chemical drugs, alcohol, or whatever is easy and quick to get just to help calm them. But, fortunately, that was not the case with Ted, as he had experienced firsthand and seen the effects played out in others' lives enough not to go that route, thankfully. So after talking to some of his friends in the tile business, he made the decision to open another business and incorporate it with men working for him and investors as partners to go after even bigger jobs. So with that in place, all seemed to be going well. I made the decision to discuss with his doctor to see if this was an inherited condition and found out it was not. So before long, I became pregnant, and our adorable little baby girl was born. It seemed like our dream was back on track.

Well, as time went on, with two children and a growing business that had become more demanding and stressful, Ted's mental health seemed to worsen. He became agitated easily and verbally abusive to me quite a bit. I found out the hard way not to argue back at him. This was something I had never before been involved in, so I cried a lot and just tried to stay out of his way and carry on life as normal as possible. The doctors tried to put him on medication to help control his mental state, but he was not having anything to do with it if it made him feel different, he said.

One day, while on a newly constructed job site, his foot rolled on a nail, causing him to fall back and hit his head on the concrete. His doctor ran a test and found a bleed in the area of the AVM. So at that point, it was decided by his neurologist to diagnose him as disabled and could not work anymore. He was then sent to cognitive therapy and put under the care of a psychiatrist for control of his mental health and medication management.

Well, where do we go from here was my thought. Do I go to work? My parents were always so supportive and knew things had been very strained. But with their strong faith-filled loving support and my tiny mustard seed of faith, which, under so much pressure, I really forgot about, I just kept putting one step ahead of the other. So I thought a change was needed and began to look for a home in the country. We put our home up for sale and could not believe it sold so fast. So I had to really step up and look a lot quicker for another home. Well, while looking, I came across a listing of acreage way out of town in the country that was at an incredible price. Ted would not agree to go look at it because he said it had to be swamp land. The developer assured me it was not, and being the kind man he was, we worked up a plan for him to call at a certain time that I knew

Ted would answer the phone. He talked him into riding out and taking a look. It was close to a four-acre track that was beautiful and high and dry—no clearing required and ready to build a home. So the deal was set. Ted even made him an offer of less than he was asking, and he took it. So it was a happy day for all, and it was not long before our brick home in the country was built. Another step in our dream direction coming alive.

With an undecided future, I thought it best that I look for more of a career job training for myself. So with two small children and a disabled husband, I went to a junior college to get my medical assistant and administrative training. I really wanted to be a nurse, but the shift work would not have been advisable with the way things were. I was also taking a parenting class at the kid's local school to connect with other mothers with children of the same age. Ted's condition had put him into depression and mental instability a lot. Well, I felt it was a challenge, but we were in the last part of our dream with two children and a home in the country. As thankful as I was, things were going to get worse, and I was fixing to see another dark side of life.

As I mentioned, with Ted's mental ability getting more unstable, he began to take his mental and physical pain out on me with verbal and physical abuse. It seemed like the harder I tried, the worse things got. He was getting the very best professional medical care he could get and was so much better seeing them. But at home, he went from Jekyll to Hyde. He broke some beautiful blown glassware that my parents had brought us from Williamsburg, Pennsylvania. He broke out windows if he did not like what I had to say about anything. He tore up my parenting class book. When I started working in the doctor's office and was responsible for transporting surgical and office equipment between two offices, he would take my car off in the middle of the night, so I was frantic as to where he was or what I would tell my doctor I worked for. Then he brings a gun to the house and threatens me with it.

I made sure I got rid of that threat and gave the gun to my father to lock up in his car trunk. Of course, that just made him more out of control. Those were such difficult times. It was like I had three children, and one was mentally unstable. It's funny looking back on that now. I was emotionally distraught but still just putting one foot in front of the other and had the strength to handle things somehow. Unfortunately, for the safety of myself and my children, I had to make a decision to get a restraining order and file for a separation. Being the codependent person I was, it was a very hard decision. After a month, though, things did settle down. Of course, I worried about him and felt no one could care for him and make sure he was keeping all his appointments like I did. The woman's attorney was eagerly pressing me to go ahead and file for a divorce. I was strong but at a loss as to what to do. Our dream wasn't supposed to end like this. When you are so weighed down and tired of the heavy load, I hit my knees and prayed for guidance.

It was summertime, and our local church was having Vacation Bible School. So I took Christie to enroll her. I was asked by a lady there if I would like to help out, as they were shorthanded. So I did. One of the crafts was to help children make a wooden heart that they would decorate and put a favorite Bible verse on it to be able to hang on their wall. So while helping with Bible verses for application on their heart wall craft, I turned to the bible and came across a verse in Psalms 196:19 that read, "Commit your way unto the Lord, trust in him, and he will direct your path." I came home and looked at my mustard seed of faith charm that Ted had given me years ago at Christmas when we were dating. I felt God was showing me the way, and I knew the answer.

That mustard seed of faith had been there all along, and I was too busy and wrapped up in life's ups and downs and the darkness in our life to realize it. That was a growing moment in my life. I grew stronger in my faith and mentally and physically with God's loving wisdom pointing me to the light. I did not go forward with the divorce. Oh, I knew it was going to be hard, but I knew I was not alone, and it was not perfect but better. I joined a gym to release stress, and Troy, our son, went fishing and hunting and spent a lot more time with his dad, which was a great help. I was the Gatorade-toting team mom for the baseball games Troy also was playing, and I stayed busy with Christie, our daughter, and her friends with horses, roller skating, 4H meetings and their projects, and shopping, of course. We even took some ribbons at one of the 4H cooking contests at Christmastime, baking a Christmas-tree cake, wreath, and candy cane cookies. We also cooked big gingerbread cookies, decorated them, and wrapped them up to hand out to their friends on Christmas Eve. Those were fun times.

Well, time passed pretty fast, and the kids grew up, and after graduating high school, they each started their own jobs and lives. I was working full-time, and the Memorial Day weekend was coming up, and I was scheduled to work. So Ted decided to ride with his sister and her husband over to their small hometown of Madison, Florida, to visit with their mother, the rest of the siblings, and their families. They had a great time, as they always did when they got together.

As the weekend progressed, another unexpected side of life happened, and Ted's brother, whom he had stayed the night with, found Ted on the floor of his bathroom. He died on the way to the hospital in the ambulance. He was forty-seven years old, and his body just could not handle his condition any longer. We were married twenty-six years, and even though our teenage dream had come true, I realized it was that mustard seed of faith that had shown us the way, especially through life's darkest times. I knew Ted was out of his mental and physical anguish. He had lived to see his children grow up and was able to spend the last few days of his life in his hometown, laughing and enjoying a loving time spent with his mom and siblings he grew up with.

So as life would have it, I have gone through a lot of seasons in my life since then that have brought me joy and happiness and pain and suffering. But what those days taught me is that a tiny seed of faith grows stronger with the things we face, and even though we are all different and have our own journeys, the light, love, and hope that comes from that tiny faith can move mountains and will change your life. I know it did mine.

About the Author

Jeanette remains in a small town in Florida on a large tract of land with her two children living close by. Their families have grown with several grandchildren, and although they all have busy lives, holidays are a special time when they all try to gather for good food, laughter and fun, and of course, some squabbles. Being the Florida girl she is, her happy place is on the East Coast beaches close to St. Augustine, with great seafood, specialty, and thrift shops. Her hobby is redoing vintage furniture to make Florida Shabby Sheek pieces with the starfish theme for her house while getting with friends and playing some pickleball. Volunteering to help feed families at Thanksgiving at her church has always been a wonderful time just to see the gratitude and happiness it brings to them all.